It's Laugh o'clock
Would you Rather?
Stocking Stuffer Edition

Funny Scenarios, Wacky Choices
and Hilarious Situations
For Kids and Family

With Fun Illustrations

Riddleland

Copyright 2021 - Riddleland All rights reserved.

The content contained within this book may not be reproduced, duplicated or transmitted without direct written permission from the author or the publisher.

By reading this document, the reader agrees that under no circumstances is the author responsible for any losses, direct or indirect, that are incurred as a result of the use of the information contained within this document, including, but not limited to, errors, omissions, or inaccuracies.

Legal Notice:
This book is copyright protected. It is only for personal use. You cannot amend, distribute, sell, use, quote or paraphrase any part, or the content within this book, without the consent of the author or publisher.

Disclaimer Notice:
Please note the information contained within this document is for educational and entertainment purposes only. All effort has been executed to present accurate, up to date, reliable, complete information. No warranties of any kind are declared or implied. Readers acknowledge that the author is not engaged in the rendering of legal, financial, medical or professional advice. The content within this book has been derived from various sources. Please consult a licensed professional before attempting any techniques outlined in this book.

Designs by freepik.com

TABLE OF CONTENTS

Introduction — pg 5

Turn it into a game — pg 7

Would You Rather? — pg 9

Did you enjoy the book? — pg 109

Bonus Book — pg 110

Contest — pg 111

Other books by Riddleland — pg 112

About Riddleland — pg 115

Riddleland Bonus

Join our **Facebook Group** at **Riddleland for Kids**
to get daily jokes and riddles.

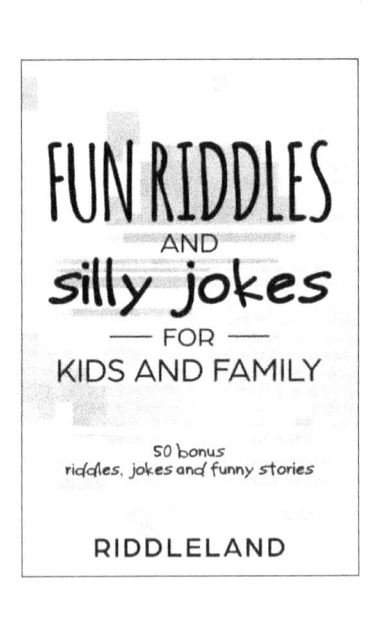

https://pixelfy.me/riddlelandbonus

Thank you for buying this book. As a token of our appreciation, we would like to offer a special bonus—a collection of 50 original jokes, riddles, and funny stories.

INTRODUCTION

"What I like about Christmas is that you can make people forget the past with the present."
~ Don Marquis

Are you ready to make some decisions? **It's Laugh O'Clock - Would You Rather? Stocking Stuffer Edition** is a collection of funny scenarios, wacky choices, and hilarious situations which offer alternative endings for kids and adults to choose between.

These questions are an excellent way to get a fun and exciting conversation started. Also, by asking "Why?" after a "Would you Rather . . . " question, learn a lot about the person, including their values and their thinking process.

We wrote this book because we want children to be encouraged to read more, think, and grow. As parents, we know that when children play games, they are being educated while having so much fun that they don't even realize they're learning and developing valuable life skills. "Would you Rather . . . " is one of our favorite games to play as a family. Some of the 'would you rather ...' scenarios have had us in fits of giggles, others have generated reactions such as: "Eeeeeeuuugh, that's gross!" and yet others really make us think, reflect and consider our own decisions.

Besides having fun, playing these questions have other benefits such as:

Enhancing Communication – This game helps children to interact, read aloud, and listen to others. It's a fun way for parents to get their children interacting with them without a formal, awkward conversation. The game can also help to get to know someone better and learn about their likes, dislikes, and values.

Building Confidence – The game encourages children to get used to pronouncing vocabulary, asking questions, and overcoming shyness.

Developing Critical Thinking – It helps children to defend and justify the rationale for their choices and can generate discussions and debates. Parents playing this game with young children can give them prompting questions about their answers to help them reach logical and sensible decisions.

Improving Vocabulary – Children will be introduced to new words in the questions, and the context of them will help them remember the words because the game is fun.

Encouraging Equality and Diversity – Considering other people's answers, even if they differ from your own, is important for respect, equality, diversity, tolerance, acceptance, and inclusivity. Some questions may get children to think outside the box and move beyond stereotypes associated with gender.

Welcome to It's Laugh O'Clock

Would You Rather?
Stocking Stuffer Edition

How do you play?

At least two players are needed to play this game. Face your opponent and decide who is **Santa 1** and **Santa 2**. If you have 3 or 4 players, you can decide which players belong to **Santa Group 1** and **Santa Group 2**. The goal of the game is to score points by making the other players laugh. The first player to a score of 10 points is the **Champion**.

What are the rules?

Santa 1 starts first. Read the questions aloud and choose an answer. The same player will then explain why they chose the answer in the silliest and wackiest way possible. If the reason makes the **Santa 2** laugh, then **Santa 1** scores a funny point. Take turns going back and forth and write down the score.

How do you get started?

Flip a coin. The Santa that guesses it correctly starts first.

Bonus Tip:
Making funny voices, silly dance moves or wacky facial expressions will make your opponent laugh!

Most Importantly:
Remember to have fun and enjoy the game!

Would You Rather...

Compete in a race where you get to ride on the back of a flying reindeer

OR

on a snowy mountain where you get to ride on skis with rockets attached to them?

Eat sushi using cinnamon sticks as chopsticks

OR

eat your entire Christmas dinner with tweezers?

Would You Rather...

Go ice skating on all fours while wearing reindeer antlers and yelling "free reindeer rides!"

OR

while wearing a polar bear costume and shouting "I'm going to eat you!"

Spend the day shopping for Christmas presents online

OR

watching Christmas movies on Netflix?

Would You Rather...

Slide down a snowy hill really fast on your belly while dressed like a penguin

OR

really slow on a sled pulled by miniature sled dog puppies?

Wrap all your Christmas presents in greasy, used Chinese food to-go boxes

OR

in doggy poo bags that have been cleaned but still smell like poo?

Would You Rather...

Wear a sparkly red nose and fuzzy antlers

OR

a velvet Santa hat and curly beard everywhere you go for one week?

Go to a concert performed by the little drummer boy

OR

a dance recital performed by the 9 ladies dancing (from the 12 Days of Christmas song)?

Would You Rather...

Go to a Christmas carnival to ride on a rollercoaster with Santa

OR

to eat red and green cotton candy with an elf?

Magically jump into your favorite Christmas book and become one of the characters

OR

have one of the characters jump out of the book to play with you?

Would You Rather...

Ride to school on the back of a giant polar bear

OR

have Santa drop you off in his sleigh?

- -

Have Santa trade places with your teacher so that he teaches your class, and your teacher delivers your Christmas presents

OR

have Santa trade places with your parents so that he tucks you into bed at night and your parents fly the sleigh?

Would You Rather...

Eat a candy cane that makes you sneeze uncontrollably for 20 minutes

OR

that gives you webbed penguin feet for a day?

- - - - - - - - - - - - - - - - -

Never be able to play in the snow again

OR

never be able to sing another Christmas song again?

Would You Rather...

Have to wear oversized, fuzzy polar bear slippers

OR

sparkly, neon ice skates to school every day for one month?

Have a huge Christmas feast with all your favorite foods by yourself

OR

skip dinner and volunteer to feed less-fortunate people with your friends?

Would You Rather...

Go hiking while wearing a backpack full of Christmas cookies that attracts polar bears

OR

long, pointy elf shoes that make you trip?

Wear your fanciest holiday clothes

OR

embarrassing footy pajamas to school for one year?

Would You Rather...

Eat a magic Christmas cookie that gives you the power to know all the answers on your math tests

OR

your spelling tests?

Have big, red poinsettias growing out of your head

OR

squishy, green gumdrops growing on your toes?

Would You Rather...

Have an ice queen cast a spell on you that gives you the power to understand every language in the entire world

OR

that gives you the power to fly as far as you want, whenever you want?

• • • • • • • • • • • • •

Go to a special zoo that lets you bottle-feed a baby reindeer

OR

that lets you play fetch with polar bear cubs?

Would You Rather...

Decorate a prickly, 12-armed saguaro cactus by putting Santa hats on each arm

OR

OR an extra-tall redwood tree by putting beach ball-sized ornaments on the branches?

Trade the traditional red and green Christmas colors for orange and blue

OR

pink and purple?

Would You Rather...

Have Santa slide down a water slide

OR

a firefighter's pole instead of a chimney?

See all the grownups in your family jumping, shouting, and getting excited like kids on Christmas morning

OR

see all the kids in your family cooking, decorating, and wrapping presents like grownups on Christmas?

Would You Rather...

Have a sleepover in a treehouse built into the world's tallest Christmas tree

OR

in an igloo built into the world's coldest glacier?

Host a dance party where everyone wears their fanciest holiday clothes

OR

a book club where everyone takes turns reading their favorite Christmas story?

Would You Rather...

Win a snowball fight against an abominable snowman who makes snowballs the size of boulders

OR

a candy cane duel against a pirate who's trying to steal your family's Christmas presents?

Play ice hockey
against a team of snow bunnies

OR

win a speed skating race against a wolf?

Would You Rather...

Donate a whole sleigh-full of awesome toys and treats to kids at the children's hospital

OR

to pets at the humane society?

Run out of icing and have to decorate your Christmas cookies with spicy guacamole

OR

onion-flavored hummus?

Would You Rather...

Eat cereal that tastes like over-baked Christmas cookies

OR

pancakes that taste like year-old candy canes?

Have Rudolph sneeze in your face

OR

have all of your family members give you a wet, sloppy kiss?

Would You Rather...

See Santa fly his sleigh with striped zebras wearing superhero capes

OR

with fluffy bunnies wearing jet packs?

Invite your family to a Christmas party at your school where everyone wears silly hats

OR

invite your classmates to come to your house for a Christmas party where everyone wears mismatched clothes?

Would You Rather...

Have your favorite celebrity

OR

your favorite teacher slide down the chimney to bring you presents if Santa needed Christmas Eve off?

Only be able to give people gifts you know they won't like

OR

not receive any gifts yourself?

Would You Rather...

Play a game of baseball where you hit sparkly ornaments instead of baseballs

OR

where you swing with a giant candy cane instead of a baseball bat?

Teach someone who's never heard of Christmas before how to decorate a Christmas tree

OR

how to bake Christmas cookies?

Would You Rather...

Only be able to talk to people while gargling hot cocoa

OR

while your mouth is full of Christmas cookies?

Have really messy hair

OR

wear an embarrassing outfit in all of your Christmas pictures?

Would You Rather...

Have to open all of your Christmas presents with your mouth

OR

while wearing oven mitts on your hands?

Accidentally send Valentine's Day cards to all your friends instead of Christmas cards

OR

get an Easter basket instead of a Christmas stocking?

Would You Rather...

Have to wrap every single thing in your bedroom with wrapping paper

OR

hang Christmas lights on every inch of the outside of your house?

Have Santa give you a can of stinky tuna fish that you have to eat

OR

a list of household chores that you have to do?

Would You Rather...

Go look at Christmas lights in your neighborhood while riding in a fancy limousine decorated with a big, red, Rudolph nose

OR

in a brand new, green convertible decorated with shiny gold garland?

Have the air at Christmas time smell like ooey-gooey cinnamon rolls

OR

freshly cut Christmas trees?

Would You Rather...

Wear a Christmas wreath as a necklace

OR

extra-large ornaments as earrings to school for one week?

Accidentally wake up at 2 o'clock on Christmas morning and have to wait 6 hours for everyone else to get up to open presents

OR

accidentally sleep through Christmas morning and have to open presents all by yourself?

Would You Rather...

Have to sing every single Christmas carol you know in front of your class

OR

wear red-and-green-striped tights to school every day for one month?

- -

Wear a puffy, pink snow suit all summer long

OR

a tiny, yellow bathing suit all winter long?

Would You Rather...

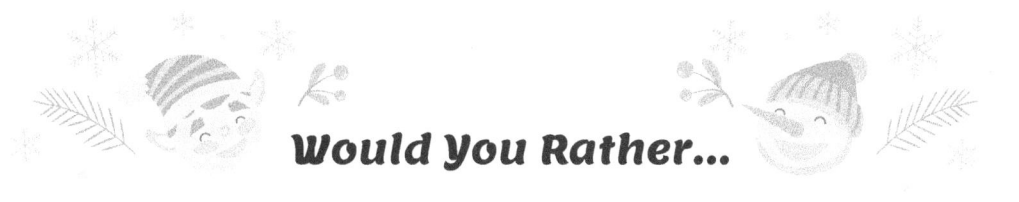

Decorate a tall palm tree on a tropical island

OR

a teeny-tiny bonsai tree in a secret forest instead of a traditional Christmas tree?

- - - - - - - - - - - - - - - - - -

Eat a candy cane covered in hot sauce

OR

a big piece of turkey covered in whipped cream?

Would You Rather...

Top your Christmas tree with a star that lights up and flashes different colors

OR

that plays your favorite Christmas songs?

Take care of a baby polar bear who likes to eat stinky fish

OR

a baby moose who likes to eat your least favorite vegetables?

Would You Rather...

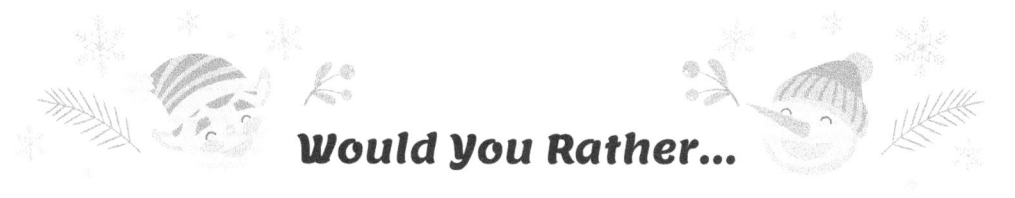

Stay up all night and see Santa putting presents under the tree

(OR)

go to bed early but you wake up to an extra present?

Add the Kwanzaa tradition of meditating

(OR)

the Hanukkah tradition of lighting a menorah to your Christmas celebrations this year?

Would You Rather...

Have your stocking filled
with 20 of your favorite candy bars

OR

with 3 of your favorite toys?

Count down to Christmas by making a list of all your
favorite holiday activities and doing one every day

OR

by getting an advent calendar and reading one part
of the Christmas story every day?

Would You Rather...

Spend the day learning how to build the coolest toys with the elves in Santa's workshop

OR

learning how to bake the yummiest cookies with Mrs. Claus in her kitchen?

Have farts that smell like peppermints

OR

burps that sound like Christmas carols?

Would You Rather...

Grow up to be a mechanic who fixes Santa's sleigh whenever it's not working properly

OR

to be a project manager who keeps track of Santa's naughty and nice lists?

Slip and fall into a pit of reindeer poop

OR

dump a hot pot of gravy on your head?

Would You Rather...

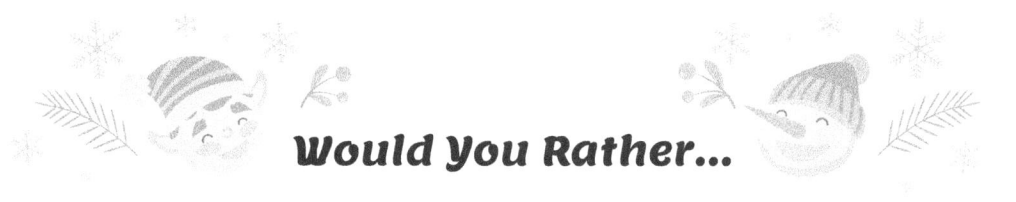

Clean up Mrs. Claus's kitchen after she spends a whole week baking Christmas cookies

OR

scoop up reindeer poop in the stables after all reindeer eat an entire field of carrots?

Stuff 100 marshmallows in your mouth

OR

100 snowballs in your mouth?

Would You Rather...

Go to a Christmas wedding where the bride tosses a bouquet of red poinsettia flowers

OR

where the groom wears a Santa suit?

Get a tummy ache every time you eat a Christmas treat

OR

a paper cut every time you unwrap a gift?

Would You Rather...

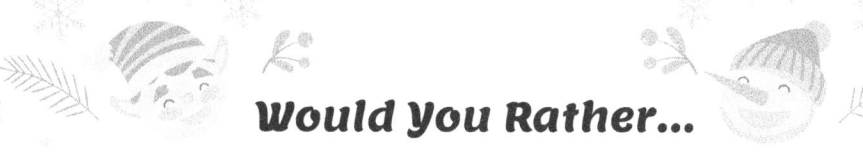

Have Santa deliver presents while riding on a metallic red motorcycle

OR

while driving a glittery green race car if his sleigh was broken on Christmas Eve?

Chug three mugs of hot cocoa in 5 minutes

OR

eat 20 candy canes in 10 minutes?

Would You Rather...

Have Santa's barber style his beard in long dreadlocks with bows on the ends

OR

in tiny braids with sparkly barrettes on the ends?

Write a 10-page book report on your favorite Christmas story

OR

do a science project where you have to figure out how to keep snow from melting in the spring?

Would You Rather...

See each of Santa's reindeer wearing bright blue combat boots

OR

pink satin ballet slippers?

See a Christmas fashion show where all the outfits are red and green, and the models are members of your family

OR

a Christmas play where the stage is made from gingerbread and the actors are your friends?

Would You Rather...

Go to a salon to get glittery candy cane stripes painted on your nails

OR

to get a red and green mohawk in your hair?

See Santa's reindeer building toys in the workshop

OR

see Santa's elves pulling the sleigh in the sky?

Would You Rather...

Have dessert with Mrs. Claus, who brings chocolate Christmas cookies,

OR

with Frosty the Snowman, who brings strawberry snow cones?

Wear a Christmas sweater that's really warm but also really itchy

OR

that's really soft but has giant holes in it?

Would You Rather...

Leave a double-bacon cheeseburger

OR

a kale salad for Santa instead of Christmas cookies?

Spend the holidays with your family by traveling to a foreign country and staying with another family in their home

OR

by having another family from a foreign country visit your home for the holidays?

Would You Rather...

Surprise Santa by leaving a present for him under your tree instead asking for a present

OR

by making him a whole chocolate pie instead of cookies?

Visit the North Pole just in time to see Santa and his reindeer taking off in his sleigh

OR

to see the Northern Lights sparkling in the sky?

Would You Rather...

Trade your most-wanted Christmas present for perfect grades on your homework for one year

OR

for a puppy that you get to name?

Wear glasses made from sticky candy canes

OR

pants made from crinkly wrapping paper?

Would You Rather...

Hang your family's Christmas stockings on a ceiling fan that's on high speed so they spin around really fast

OR

on each family member's door handle and have them fall off every time you open the door?

Have it snow every day for one year

OR

not snow once all year long?

Would You Rather...

Open all your Christmas presents one week early

OR

one week late?

Unstick your tongue from a giant icicle by pulling so hard that it stretches down to your belly button

OR

by pouring hot chocolate all over it and burning it so badly that you have to wear a bandage?

Would You Rather...

Celebrate outside at a park with decorated Christmas trees everywhere you look

OR

at a fancy hotel with beautiful Christmas wreaths on every door?

Receive a bunch of yummy candy

OR

a bunch of silly hats for Christmas?

Would You Rather...

Go to a Christmas tree lot to pick out the tallest

OR

the tiniest Christmas tree you can find?

Go hiking on a giant glacier with a moose who burps every time it talks

OR

ride a snowmobile across the tundra with a puffin who keeps singing your least-favorite Christmas song?

Would You Rather...

Get one present a day on each of the
12 days of Christmas

OR

get 12 presents all at once on Christmas Day?

• • • • • • • • • • • • • •

Take Christmas pictures with giant chunks of fruitcake
stuck in your teeth

OR

with a candy cane sticking out of your nose?

Would You Rather...

Have Santa bring you the coolest new phone

OR

a cute fluffy kitten for Christmas?

Accompany Santa in a submarine under the sea to take Christmas presents to magic mermaids

OR

in a rocket ship to outer space to take Christmas presents to friendly aliens?

Would You Rather...

Decorate the inside of your house with colorful lights

OR

the outside of your house with shiny tree ornaments?

Peek at all your Christmas presents and not get caught

OR

be completely surprised by everything you get?

Would You Rather...

See a team of tortoises wearing Santa hats

OR

a group of koalas wearing antlers leading Santa's sleigh instead of the reindeer?

Exchange Christmas cards with a kid from another country

OR

exchange Christmas ornaments with a kid who lives in your neighborhood?

Would You Rather...

Find teriyaki-flavored beef jerky

OR

salt and vinegar potato chips in your stocking instead of toys and candy?

Do a TikTok video dressed like a nutcracker who likes to salsa dance

OR

like a hockey player who likes to do eating challenges?

Would You Rather...

Give up all your Christmas presents for an all-expenses paid vacation to a tropical island for two weeks

OR

for your teacher to let you skip all of your tests and homework for one month?

Meet a snowman who likes to rap

OR

a gingerbread man who likes to sing opera?

Would You Rather...

Play a joke on your family by putting gooey macaroni and cheese in their Christmas stockings

OR

by re-wrapping the presents you gave them last year and putting them under the Christmas tree?

Offer to cook 20 turkeys

OR

to wrap 50 presents?

Would You Rather...

Have a contest with your friends to see who can hula hoop the most times with a Christmas wreath

OR

to see who can pole vault the highest using a cinnamon stick?

Tell Santa what you'd like for Christmas on a Zoom call

OR

by sitting on his lap?

Would You Rather...

Go outside and play in snow made from tiny marshmallows

OR

out of powdered sugar?

Have a sleepover with your friends in a life-sized gingerbread house, but forest animals keep eating the walls

OR

in an igloo, but your pillow is stuffed with freezing cold ice cubes?

Would You Rather...

Wear oversized oven mitts instead of mittens

OR

an itchy Christmas tree garland instead of a scarf all winter long?

Give your family and friends Christmas cookies with a secret ingredient of pointy toenail clippings

OR

sticky ear wax?

Would You Rather...

Have an extra bushy, pink Christmas tree

OR

a spindly orange Christmas tree in your house?

• • • • • • • • • • • • • • • • • •

Give Santa a new look by designing a bright red tuxedo for him instead of his traditional suit

OR

by shaving his face instead of grooming his classic white beard and mustache?

Would You Rather...

Celebrate by going to a Christmas party at a mansion where everyone drinks eggnog out of expensive, crystal glasses

OR

at a pet store where everyone drinks apple cider out of fishbowls?

Only eat candy canes

OR

only drink eggnog for one week?

Would You Rather...

Eat Christmas cookies topped with spicy jalapeños instead of sprinkles

OR

drink hot cocoa topped with sour cream instead of whipped cream?

See Santa deliver presents while riding on the back of a giant, green dragon

OR

while driving a super-fast flying car?

Would You Rather...

Have all your Christmas presents wrapped in toilet paper

OR

in trash bags?

- - - - - - - - - - - - - - -

See someone's grandma actually get run over by a reindeer, but she walks away with a hoof-shaped bruise

OR

be given a real hippopotamus for Christmas, but it lives in your room and sleeps in your bed?

Would You Rather...

Wear a nice, elegant sweater to an ugly Christmas sweater party

OR

an ugly, tacky sweater to a fancy Christmas party?

Have the Three Wise Men teach your math class how to do complicated math problems

OR

have Rudolph teach your physical education class how to run really fast?

Would You Rather...

Have to ring jingle bells every time you hear someone else say "merry Christmas"

OR

do a silly dance every time someone else says "happy holidays?"

Not get any Christmas presents this year

OR

not get any Christmas desserts this year?

Would You Rather...

Be an actor in your school's holiday Christmas play dressed as a nutcracker wearing a swimsuit

OR

as a gingerbread cookie wearing a giant cowboy hat?

Get stuck in an elevator with a family of elves who keep singing "I Want a Hippopotamus for Christmas"

OR

with a herd of reindeer who keep pooping?

Would You Rather...

Sleep on a bed of pokey pine needles

OR

on a bed of slushy ice?

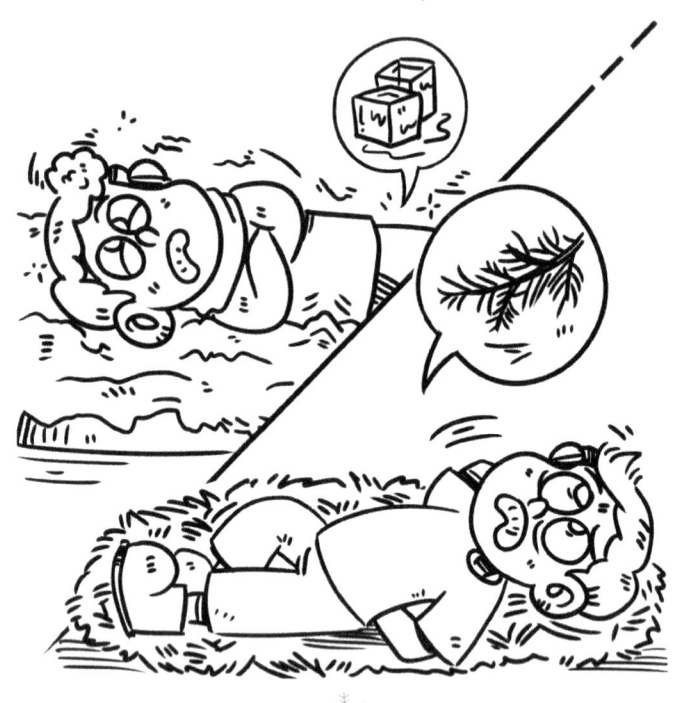

• • • • • • • • • • • • • • • • • • • •

Watch a YouTube tutorial about how to make unbreakable Christmas tree ornaments with things you can find around your house

OR

about how to build a snow fort that can withstand any snowball fight?

Would You Rather...

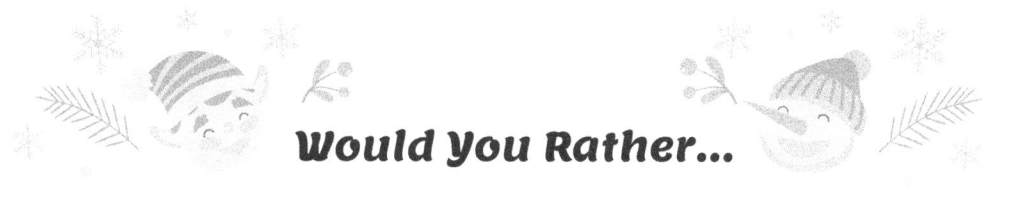

Adopt a pet penguin who likes to wear plaid suits

OR

a pet polar bear who likes to wear polka-dotted snow boots?

Have Christmas on a farm where all the animals sing Christmas carols

OR

at a cabin where every tree in the forest is decorated like a Christmas tree?

Would You Rather...

Eat a salad made with holly leaves and cranberries

OR

a soup made with pinecones and chestnuts?

Have Santa give you an untraditional gift of knowledge where you magically learn every language in the world

OR

know all the answers to your homework for the rest of your life?

Would You Rather...

Play knights with your family using icicles as swords

OR

play ninjas with your friends using snowflakes as ninja stars?

Win a snowboarding race against all of Santa's reindeer

OR

a snowball fight against a team of snowmen?

Would You Rather...

Help Santa pick out who to put on the naughty list

OR

the nice list?

Take Christmas pictures with your family while wearing flannel pajamas and making goofy faces

OR

while wearing the fanciest clothes you own and making serious faces?

Would You Rather...

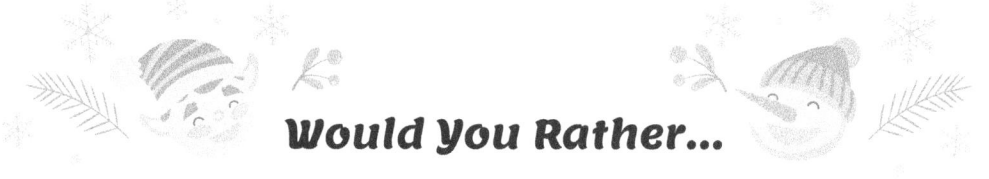

Spend an entire month wearing a wig on your head made from shiny, silver tinsel

OR

a bow on your bottom made from sparkly, red ribbon?

Do a TikTok video where you get to breakdance in the snow with all 9 reindeer

OR

do ballet in Santa's Workshop with all the elves?

Would You Rather...

Only be able to watch the same Christmas movie repeatedly

OR

not be allowed to watch any holiday movies all season long?

Say "feliz Navidad" (Spanish)

OR

"mele Kalikamaka" (Hawaiian) instead of "merry Christmas" all season long?

Would You Rather...

Eat a whole plate of Christmas cookies that were made with salt instead of sugar

OR

with toothpaste instead of frosting?

Have Frosty the Snowman teach you how to bring snow people to life

OR

have Rudolph teach you how to fly?

Would You Rather...

Go to a circus where the clowns wear Santa suits and juggle pinecones

OR

where the trapeze artists wear candy cane-striped leggings and swing on ropes made from licorice?

Have Santa's itchy, white beard

OR

big, jolly belly?

Would You Rather...

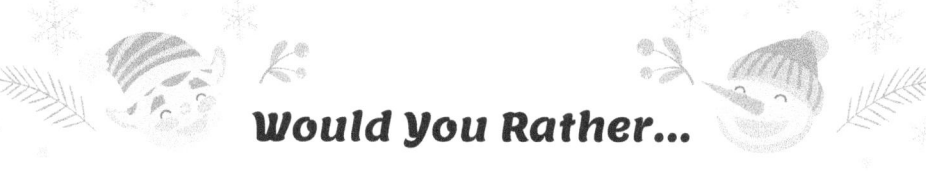

See Santa trade his hat and suit for a beanie and ripped jeans

OR

a tiara and a tutu?

Go Christmas shopping at a toy store that lets you play with all the toys before you buy them

OR

at a virtual store that lets you play fun Christmas games online before checking out?

Would You Rather...

Be put on the nice list for eating all your vegetables

OR

for cleaning your room every day for an entire year?

Have teeth made of rainbow-colored Christmas lights

OR

fingernails made from crumbly gingerbread?

Would You Rather...

Pick out your Christmas tree in the forest and cut it down with a slippery pizza cutter

OR

a sticky pair of scissors?

Take a bath in a tub filled with gooey cranberry sauce

OR

in a tub filled with sticky eggnog?

Would You Rather...

Trade places with Santa and have him sit on your lap to tell you what he wants for Christmas

OR

with the reindeer and let them ride in the sleigh while you pull it?

Have a sleepover with a walrus who wears silly footy pajamas, but snores loudly

OR

an arctic fox who eats most of the snacks but tells funny jokes in his sleep?

Would You Rather...

Lose your memory and forget to buy presents for everyone on your gift list

OR

accidentally mix up your gift tags and give everyone the wrong gifts?

Have a speed-skating race with rusty ice skates

OR

a snow-tubing race with a tube that's leaking air?

Would You Rather...

Spend an entire week stuck in a giant snow globe

OR

only being able to sit down if you rock on a rocking horse?

Grow a pair of elf ears with 7 dangly earrings on each ear

OR

a pair of moose antlers decorated with Christmas lights?

Would You Rather...

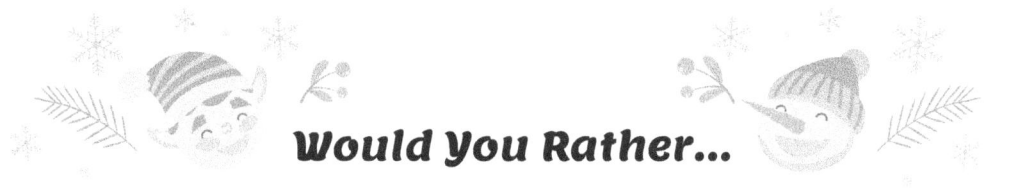

Have the power to freeze water into ice

OR

to melt snow into water?

Have an allergy to eggnog that makes your lips swell up so big they touch your nose

OR

an allergy to Christmas cookies that causes an itchy rash on your whole body?

Would You Rather...

Have a long, orange carrot nose

OR

brown, bark-covered stick arms?

• • • • • • • • • • • • • •

Grow up to be a world-class photographer who takes pictures of kids sitting on Santa's lap

OR

an expert toy engineer who teaches Santa's elves how to make toys?

Would You Rather...

Wear pants made from Christmas wreaths that make you walk funny

OR

a wig made from ribbons that curl every time you brush your hair?

Play hockey with giant candy canes instead of hockey sticks

OR

play tennis with pinecones instead of tennis balls?

Would You Rather...

Have Santa think he's the Easter Bunny and leave candy-filled Easter eggs in your stocking

OR

think he's the Tooth Fairy and make Christmas ornaments out of your baby teeth?

Grow up to be an expert gift wrapper

OR

a professional reindeer trainer?

Would You Rather...

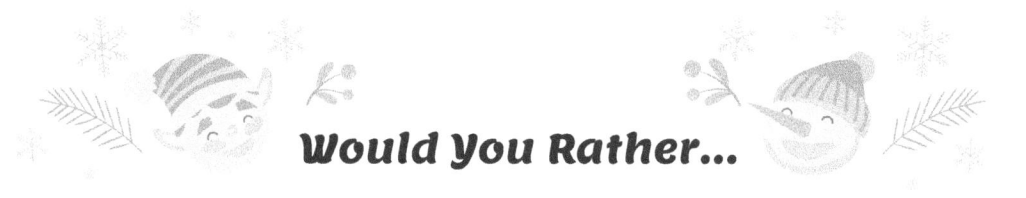

Get warmed up after playing in the snow by standing under a giant blow dryer at a car wash

OR

by taking a bath in hot chocolate?

Shovel snow for all your neighbors all winter long

OR

wrap all of your neighbors' Christmas presents for them?

Would You Rather...

Have a Christmas treat exchange with the Queen of England, who gives you a plate of cranberry biscuits

OR

with the President of the United States, who gives you an apple pie?

Exercise by running like Rudolph

OR

by lifting a barbell made from giant peppermints?

Would You Rather...

Have magic powers that let you build a snowman during summertime

OR

that let you grow a flower garden during winter?

Have to clean up after Christmas dinner all by yourself

OR

have to put all of the Christmas decorations away by yourself?

Would You Rather...

Do figure-8s at an ice-skating rink while driving an ice resurfacing machine

OR

smash through a snowbank in your neighborhood with a snowplow?

Go bowling where you use a giant snowball as your bowling ball

OR

where you use tiny Christmas trees as bowling pins?

Would You Rather...

Read your favorite Christmas story of all time to your class

OR

make up a new Christmas story and act it out with your friends?

Have to spend an entire day cracking nuts with a nutcracker that gives you splinters

OR

untangling Christmas lights that shock you?

Would You Rather...

Have a "secret Santa" gift exchange with the kids in your class, where everyone gets a present but doesn't know who it's from

OR

a "white elephant" gift exchange with your family, where each person takes a turn picking a mystery gift from a big group of presents?

Drink a pinecone milkshake

OR

eat a peppermint pizza?

Would You Rather...

Help Santa on Christmas Eve by holding glowing batons on the runway to help his sleigh take off and land safely

OR

by feeding the reindeer carrots in the stables so they have a healthy meal before flying around the world?

Have a Christmas tree in every room in your house

OR

not have a Christmas tree at all?

Would You Rather...

Collect a teeny-tiny snow globe

OR

a funny-shaped Christmas ornament each time you visit a new place?

Go Christmas shopping with a grandma who makes you try on every piece of clothing in the mall

OR

with a friend who forgets their wallet and asks you to pay for everything?

Would You Rather...

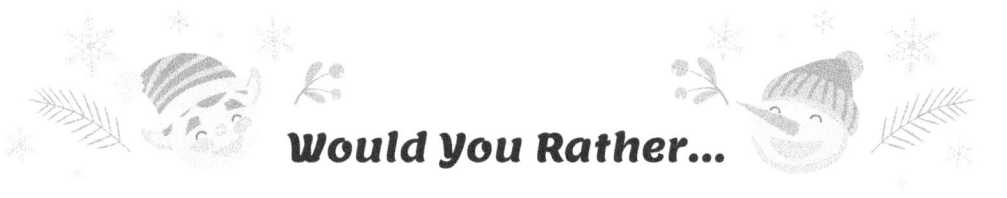

Have to wear red, polka-dotted long underwear instead of regular clothes

OR

fuzzy, fleece socks instead of shoes every day from now until Christmas?

Get in trouble for eating all of Santa's Christmas cookies

OR

for peeking at all your Christmas presents?

Would You Rather...

Turn into a goose and fly south for the winter

OR

turn into a bear and hibernate all winter?

Go to a Christmas party while wearing your underwear over your clothes

OR

go to a sleepover while wearing long johns with a butt flap that keeps coming unbuttoned?

Would You Rather...

Get five dollars every time someone says "Bah, humbug!"

OR

your favorite candy bar every time someone says "Ho, ho, ho!"

Only be able to sing "Jingle Bells" and no other Christmas carols

OR

not sing any Christmas carols all season long?

Would You Rather...

Spread Christmas cheer by telling funny Christmas jokes to your class

OR

by giving new yo-yos to grumpy adults?

Post an Instagram story while holding a sled dog puppy who's licking your face

OR

while going on a fast sleigh ride in the snow with your friends?

Would You Rather...

Eat your entire Christmas dinner without using any silverware

OR

clean up after dinner without using the dishwasher?

Go camping in an igloo with one of Santa's elves who brings you a toy

OR

stay in a fancy hotel with a gingerbread man who comes to life?

Would You Rather...

Get in the Christmas spirit by coloring red and green pictures for everyone in your family

OR

by baking cranberry cupcakes for all your friends?

Pick out a new ornament with your closest family member at your favorite toy store

OR

watch a tree lighting with your best friend in your favorite park?

Would You Rather...

Complete a class project where you have to make an ice sculpture of your favorite animal

OR

build a snowman that looks like your teacher?

• • • • • • • • • • • • • • • • • • • •

Drive a dogsled with a pack of fluffy puppies who keep tripping over themselves

OR

a pack of vicious guard dogs who slobber all over the sled?

Would You Rather...

Have a race with your friends to see who's fastest at making 100 snow angels

OR

fastest at eating 100 Christmas cookies?

Go swimming with a narwhal who teaches you how to hold your breath for one hour

OR

a seal who teaches you how to do underwater backflips?

Would You Rather...

Serve toilet water

OR

cough syrup with Santa's cookies if you run out of milk?

• • • • • • • • • • • • • • • • • • • •

Eat your entire Christmas dinner while standing up on your chair while everyone else sits down

OR

while sitting underneath the table and begging for scraps like a dog?

Would You Rather...

Catch snowflakes on your tongue that taste like rotten eggs

OR

moldy cheese?

- - - - - - - - - - -

Get two of your most-wanted Christmas presents and give one to your best friend

OR

to a kid you don't know who doesn't get a Christmas present this year?

Did You Enjoy The Book ?

If you did, we are ecstatic. If not, please write your complaint to us and we will ensure we fix it.

If you're feeling generous, there is something important that you can help me with – tell other people that you enjoyed the book.

Ask a grown-up to write about it on Amazon. When they do, more people will find out about the book. It also lets Amazon know that we are making kids around the world laugh. Even a few words and ratings would go a long way.

If you have any ideas or jokes that you think are super funny, please let us know. We would love to hear from you.

Our email address is -
riddleland@riddlelandforkids.com

Riddleland Bonus

Join our **Facebook Group** at **Riddleland for Kids** to get daily jokes and riddles.

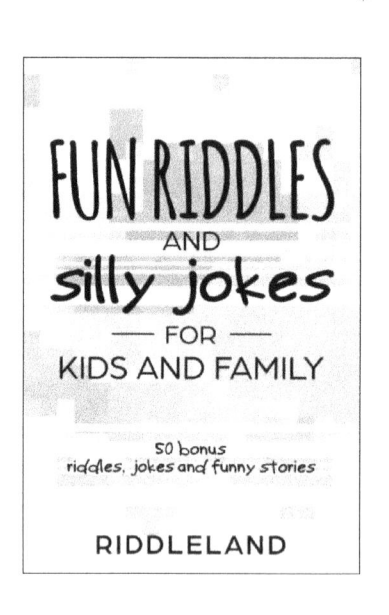

https://pixelfy.me/riddlelandbonus

Thank you for buying this book. As a token of our appreciation, we would like to offer a special bonus—a collection of 50 original jokes, riddles, and funny stories.

CONTEST

Would you like your jokes and riddles to be featured in our next book?

We are having a contest to discover the cleverest and funniest boys and girls in the world!

1) Creative and Challenging Riddles
2) Tickle Your Funny Bone Contest

Parents, please email us your child's "original" riddle or joke. He or she could win a Riddleland book and be featured in our next book.

Here are the rules:

1) We're looking for super challenging riddles and extra funny jokes.

2) Jokes and riddles MUST be 100% original—NOT something discovered on the Internet.

3) You can submit both a joke and a riddle because they are two separate contests.

4) Don't get help from your parents—UNLESS they're as funny as you are.

5) Winners will be announced via email or our Facebook group – **Riddleland for kids**

6) In your entry, please confirm which book you purchased.

Email us at **Riddleland@riddlelandforkids.com**

Other Fun Books by Riddleland
Riddles Series

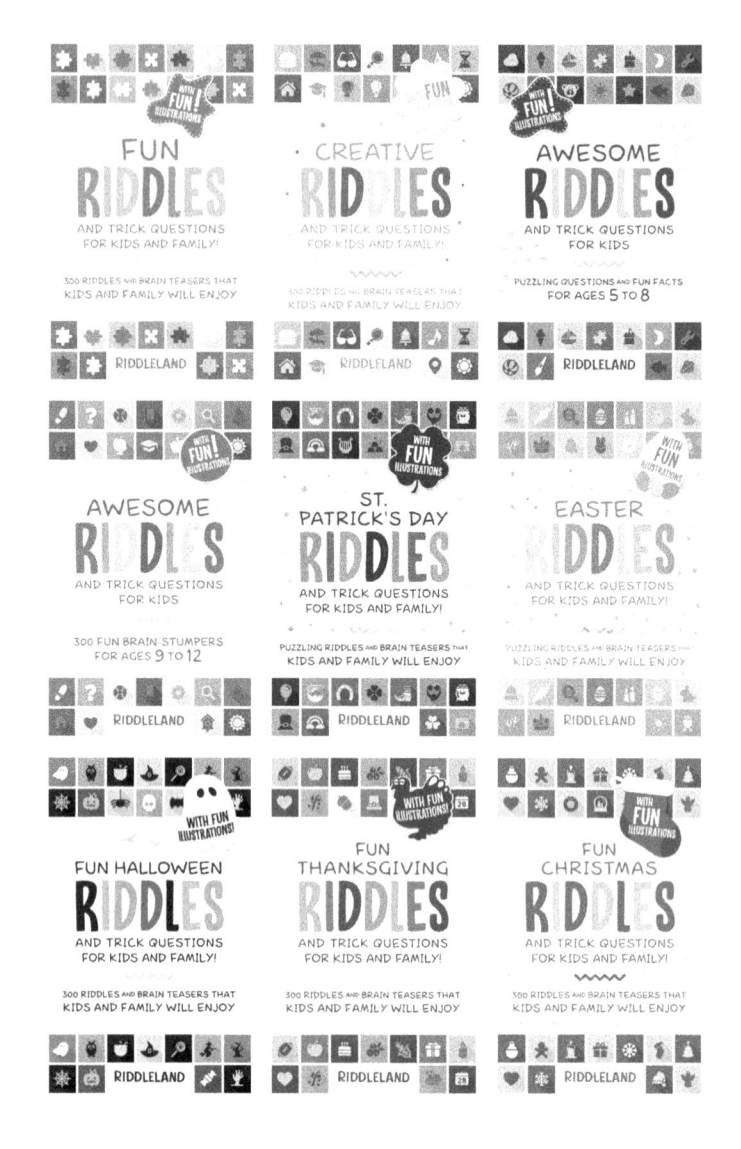

It's Laugh O'Clock Joke Books

Would You Rather...Series

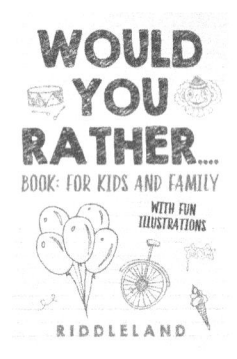

Get them on Amazon or our website at
www.riddlelandforkids.com

ABOUT RIDDLELAND

Riddleland is a mum + dad run publishing company. We are passionate about creating fun and innovative books to help children develop their reading skills and fall in love with reading. If you have suggestions for us or want to work with us, shoot us an email at

riddleland@riddlelandforkids.com

Our favourite family quote

"Creativity is an area in which younger people have a tremendous advantage since they have an endearing habit of always questioning past wisdom and authority."

– Bill Hewlett

CPSIA information can be obtained
at www.ICGtesting.com
Printed in the USA
BVHW031725121222
654044BV00010B/577